Making Music

Written by Mark Ormerod
Illustrated by Jo Taylor

Electric instruments

Nowadays, you can hear a lot of electric instruments in all kinds of music.

Electric guitar

Electric violin

Electric keyboard

Electronic drums

But some people prefer the sound of non-electric, acoustic instruments. Let's look at seven non-electric instruments which are popular in different countries.

The fiddle

This man is playing the fiddle, a popular instrument in Ireland.

The fiddle is a string instrument. It is a type of violin. You can hear the fiddle in traditional Irish music.

Did you know …?

Sherlock Holmes, the famous detective, played the violin.

Steel drums

These people are playing steel drums, a popular instrument in Trinidad and Tobago, in the Caribbean.

The steel drum is a percussion instrument. You can hear the sound of steel drums in calypso music.

Did you know …?

Steel drums are made from oil drums.

Bagpipes

This man is playing the bagpipes, a popular instrument in Scotland.

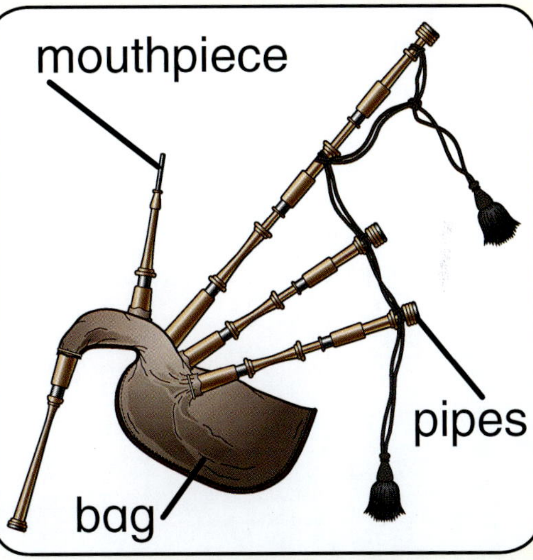

The bagpipes are a wind instrument. You can hear the bagpipes in traditional Scottish music.

Did you know …?

You can see a lot of bagpipe players in The Trooping of the Colour ceremony, in London.

The gong

These men are playing the gong, a popular instrument in China.

Gongs are percussion instruments. You can hear the gong in Chinese opera and musical theatre.

Did you know …?

In Japan, sumo wrestling competitions start with the sound of a gong.

The harp

This woman is playing the harp, a popular instrument in Ireland.

The harp is a string instrument. You can hear it in traditional Irish music.

Did you know ...?

You can see a picture of a harp on Irish euro coins.

The sitar

This woman is playing the sitar, a popular instrument in India.

The sitar is a string instrument. You can hear it in Hindi pop music and Bollywood musicals.

Did you know …?

A part of the sitar is made from a type of pumpkin.

Pan pipes

These musicians are playing pan pipes, a popular instrument in Peru.

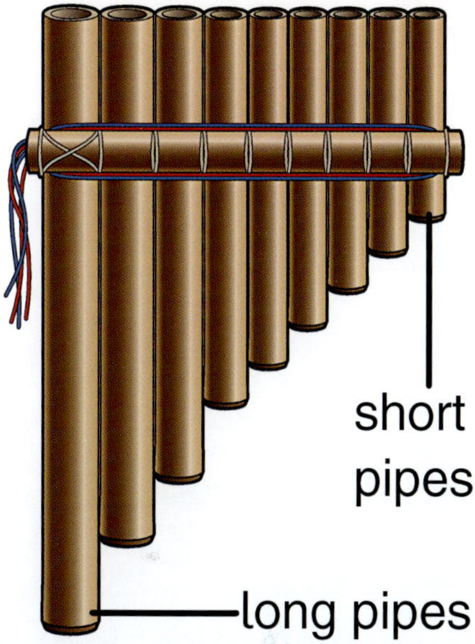

The pan pipes are a wind instrument. You can hear them in traditional Peruvian music.

Did you know ...?

Pan pipes are made from bamboo.

Your favourite instruments

Listen to the music around you – on the internet, at concerts, on television, on the radio and in the street. What instruments can you hear?

Do you prefer electric or acoustic instruments?

What are your favourite musical instruments?

The Talent Contest

The Fairness Talent
Contest for Musicians
Can you play a musical
instrument?
Come to Fairness School
on Saturday evening
at 7 o'clock.
First Prize

Written by Mark Ormerod
Illustrated by Jo Taylor

It's four o'clock in the town of Fairness.
Jack and all the children are leaving school.

Bye, Jack.
Fairness School
See you tomorrow.

As Jack walks home, he plays his recorder.

TOYS
Music

He stops to read a poster in front of the music shop.

irness
Shop
The Fairness Talent Contest for Musicians
Can you play a musical instrument?
Come to Fairness School on Saturday evening at 7 o'clock.
First Prize

Teddy and Trish come out of the music shop.

Look, Jack. I've got a new electric guitar.
I've got a new electric keyboard.

Teddy and Trish are rude to Jack.

You can't win the talent contest.
Contest for Musicians
Can you play a musical instrument?
No, you play the recorder.

Now Jack is upset.

Hi, Jack.
Hello, Sinita.
What's the matter?
I want to enter the talent contest, but I can't win with a recorder.

The next day at school, the children see their friends, Grace and Paul.

What are you doing?
We're listening to Teddy and Trish. Look!

They all watch Teddy and Trish through the music room window.

They're very good musicians.
They play very well.

Now Paul and Grace are upset.

What's the matter?
Contest for Musicians
Can you play a musical instrument?
Come to Fairness School on Saturday evening at 7 0'clock.
First Prize
I can't win the talent contest with my violin.
And I can't win with my drums.

But Sinita has a good idea.

Let's form a band. We can win the talent contest together.

It's 8 o'clock on Saturday evening. Many people are watching the talent contest.

They listen to a piano player ... and then a saxophone player.

They listen to a bagpipe player, a trumpet player and a girl with a harp. They listen to a violin player and two children with gongs.

The next musicians are Teddy and Trish.

Talent Contest
Teddy plays the electric guitar and Trish plays the electric keyboard.

Teddy and Trish are very good.

They're fantastic.

Behind the stage, Jack finds a CD player.

Grace, look! The music is coming from this CD player.
Let's turn it off.

The music stops, but Teddy and Trish continue performing.

He isn't playing the guitar.
She isn't playing the keyboard.
They're cheating!

Teddy and Trish leave the stage.

Talent Contest
You are cheating.
You're disqualified.
Boo!

The presenter introduces the final act.

Please welcome Jack,
Sinita, Grace and Paul.
They play the recorder,
the guitar, the drums
and the violin.

First, Grace starts to play the drums.

Then Paul plays the violin.

Then Sinita plays the guitar.

Finally, Jack plays the recorder.

Together, the band sounds fantastic.

Everybody loves the music. Everybody claps and cheers.

Hooray!
Hooray!

Jack, Sinita, Grace and Paul are the winners. On Sunday, their picture is in the newspaper.

This is all your fault, Teddy.
The Fairness News
Four Friends Win the Fairness Talent Contest for Musicians
Grr! It was your idea, Trish.

On Monday, a famous TV presenter visits the school. She talks to Jack, Sinita, Grace and Paul.

Congratulations on winning. This is an extra prize for you.
What is it?

It's an invitation to *The UK Talent Contest for Musicians* in July. It's on TV.
This is
INVITATION
to participate in
The UK Talent Contest
for Musicians
20th July at the
Television
Good luck! You're a very talented band.

Activities

1 Find, circle and match.

1

2

3
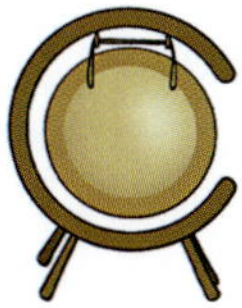

4

x	b	g	u	i	t	a	r	w
k	e	y	b	o	a	r	d	f
s	g	o	n	g	z	v	w	i
m	u	y	j	h	u	h	n	d
n	i	b	i	a	x	b	r	d
s	i	t	a	r	d	y	s	l
s	a	x	o	p	h	o	n	e
z	b	a	g	p	i	p	e	s

5

6

7

8

2 Read and circle the correct word.

1 The fiddle is a *string* / *wind* / *percussion* instrument.

2 The sitar is a *string* / *wind* / *percussion* instrument.

3 The steel drums are a *string* / *wind* / *percussion* instrument.

4 The harp is a *string* / *wind* / *percussion* instrument.

5 The pan pipes are a *string* / *wind* / *percussion* instrument.

6 The gong is a *string* / *wind* / *percussion* instrument.

3 Write the countries. Draw and colour the flags.

1 The harp is a popular instrument in Ireland.

2 The sitar is a popular instrument in ______________ .

3 The bagpipes are a popular instrument in ______________ .

4 The gong is a popular instrument in ______________ .

5 The pan pipes are a popular instrument in ______________ .

6 The fiddle is a popular instrument in ______________ .

4 Read and match the columns to make sentences.

1 The sitar	is a type of violin.
2 The fiddle	is shown on Irish euro coins.
3 Steel drums	are made from bamboo.
4 The pan pipes	are made from oil drums.
5 The harp	is made from a type of pumpkin.

5 Complete the sentence.

My favourite instruments are the ______________________
and the ______________________ .

6 Who says it? Match the speech bubbles to the characters.

1 I've got a new electric keyboard.

2 Let's form a band. We can win the talent contest together.

3 I can't win the talent contest with my violin.

4 You can't win the talent contest.

5 Good luck. You're a very talented band.

6 You're disqualified!

7 It's on TV.

8 Let's turn it off.

a 

b 

c 

d 

e 

f 

g 

h 

7 Complete the crossword.

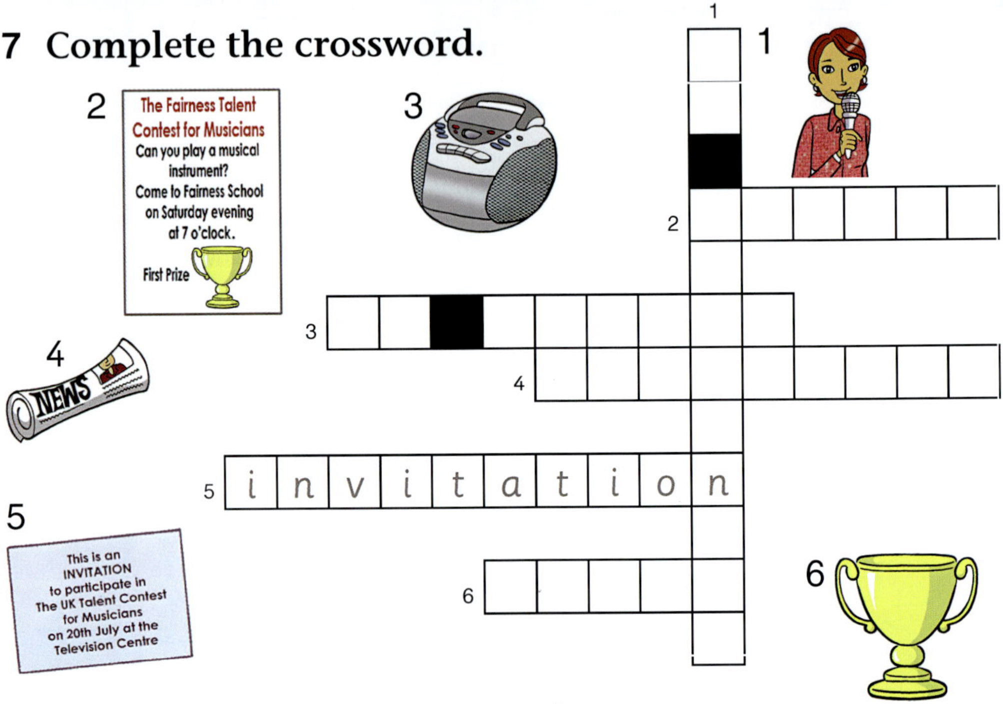

The Fairness Talent Contest for Musicians
Can you play a musical instrument?
Come to Fairness School on Saturday evening at 7 o'clock.
First Prize
NEWS
This is an INVITATION to participate in The UK Talent Contest for Musicians on 20th July at the Television Centre
i n v i t a t i o n

8 Number the sentences in order.

1 Teddy and Trish are disqualified. ☐

2 The presenter introduces Teddy and Trish. 1

3 The presenter introduces Jack, Sinita, Grace and Paul. ☐

4 A famous TV presenter gives the band an extra prize. ☐

5 Grace turns the CD player off. ☐

6 Jack, Sinita, Grace and Paul win the contest. ☐

7 Everybody claps and cheers for Jack, Sinita, Grace and Paul. ☐

9 Write the words in order to make sentences.

1 play / Sinita / guitar / the / can

Sinita can play the guitar.

2 Paul / violin / can / the / play

____

3 can't / electric / the / play / Teddy / guitar

____

4 recorder / the / can / Jack / play

____

5 Trish / play / electric / can't / keyboard / the

____

10 Write the musical instruments from the story.

1 b a g p i p e s

2 d _ _ _ _

3 e _ _ _ _ _ _ _ _ g _ _ _ _ _ _

4 e _ _ _ _ _ _ _ _ k _ _ _ _ _ _ _ _

5 g _ _ _ _ _

6 g _ _ _

7 h _ _ _

8 p _ _ _ _

9 r _ _ _ _ _ _ _

10 s _ _ _ _ _ _ _ _ _

11 t _ _ _ _ _ _ _

12 v _ _ _ _ _

Picture Dictionary

electric keyboard

opera

television

pumpkin

coin

drums

violin

recorder

guitar

newspaper

music shop

room

window

leave school

prize

It's four o'clock.

It's eight o'clock.

The Fairness Talent
Contest for Musicians
Can you play a musical instrument?
Come to Fairness School
on Saturday evening
at 7 o'clock.
First Prize

poster

upset

rude

TV presenter

piano player

trumpet player

saxophone player

stage

band

clap

Hooray!

cheer

win

On
Off

turn off

CD player

town

Macmillan Education Limited
4 Crinan Street
London N1 9XW

Companies and representatives throughout the world

ISBN 978-1-3800-3841-8

First published 2011
This edition published 2019

Illustrated by Peter Harper and Jo Taylor

The author and publishers would like to thank the following for permission to reproduce their photographic material:

Cover Photography with the kind permission of Getty Images/ Image Bank (cover, back cover).

Alamy Stock Photo/LightField Studios Inc. p10(t), Getty Images/Ablestock.com p8(tl), Alamy/Neil McAllister p9(tl), Alamy Stock Photo/Indiapicture p8(tl), Alamy/Keith Morris p7(tl), Alamy/PJC Studio p7(br), Alamy/Scouting Stock p2(cr), Alamy/Martin Thomas p3(l), Alamy/Paul Thompson Images p5(tl) Alamy Stock Photo/Tim Graham p5 (br); **BrandX Pictures** p2(tl); **Corbis**/Antenna / fstop p10(br), Corbis/Macduff Everton p6(tl); **Getty Images** p1, Getty Images/Ablestock.com p2(tr), Getty Images/The Image Bank p4(tl); **Macmillan Publishers Ltd** p2(bl).

Printed and bound in Argentina

2021
3